High Fives and A Big Heart

Written and Illustrated by Jeffrey and his 4th Grade Friends

Having a brother with Down syndrome can be difficult and frustrating because he doesn't always listen to me, but it is also nice because Jeff is really funny. Everyone at Alexandria Middle School knows Jeff. He is friends with everyone. He probably knows more people than I do. I think the book is a great way to tell people about Down syndrome because I never thought of it as being a big deal. He does everything everyone else does. He plays sports on the same teams as the other kids; he's just as good. Jeffrey is just like any other person and does what everyone else does. I really like the title of the book because it is very true! Jeff has a big heart and he gives ~ and deserves ~ a lot of high fives!

~ *Michael Bill (Jeffrey's older brother)*

As teachers, we encourage our students to share their talents and gifts with others. In our fourth grade classroom, Jeffrey was always demonstrating his terrific sense of humor, athletic ability (especially when playing kickball), and willingness to help others. Jeffrey's enthusiasm for being part of a team was contagious, and his happy spirit brightened the whole classroom. We would like to give Jeffrey a big high five for having such a big heart and for sharing his gifts with others!

~ *Michele Petrie & Susanna DeWire (Jeffrey's 4th grade teachers)*

High Fives and A Big Heart
Copyright © 2012 Jeffrey and his 4th Grade Friends
Edited by Kimberly Resh (Mikayla's mom)
ISBN: 978-0-615-53883-9
First edition, 2012

Mikayla's Voice
PO Box 232, Nazareth, PA 18064
www.mikaylasvoice.org
610.746.2323

A big high five to Jeffrey and his family who taught us to appreciate our differences and value our friendships.

Jeffrey's nickname is Jeff

and he is a 4th grader at Alexandria Middle School.

He is a tall boy with short light brown hair

and green eyes who smiles a lot.

He high fives people in the hallway,

gives lots of hugs, and has billions of friends.

The whole fourth grade loves Jeffrey.

At our school we always have pizza on Fridays.

Jeffrey's favorite food is pizza with ketchup on it.

Some people think that's weird

and you might be thinking that's gross,

but maybe to him that's yummy.

It must taste good to him.

He puts ketchup on all his food, mostly, except eggs.

We think that's odd but in a good way.

Everybody is different.

Jeffrey Daniel Bill was born August 9, 2000,
on a Wednesday. Before he was born his parents
were going to name him either Tyler or Christopher,
but instead they named him Jeffrey.

He looked like a Jeffrey.

He got his middle name from his Uncle Danny
because he was the first one to see him after he was born.

When Jeffrey was born he had

a tiny, tiny hole in his heart.

It looked small but for a hole in his heart it was huge.

It was a big deal and his mom and dad were really scared.

Jeffrey was only eight months old when the doctors

closed the hole and fixed his heart.

After surgery he had to stay in the hospital for ten days.

Jeffrey has a scar down the center of his chest,

but you only see it when he goes swimming.

Now his heart is fine.

It doesn't stop him from running around and having fun.

Outside recess is Jeffrey's favorite because
he loves the monkey bars and jumping off of them.

He is an expert at the monkey bars.

We like to hang out with Jeffrey at recess and play sports
like basketball, wall ball, frisbee, tag and kickball.
If you are ever on the opposite kickball team from Jeffrey
you stand no chance because when he kicks
it goes all the way to the outfield.

Jeffrey is an incredible athlete.

He loves to play sports and luckily is great at them.

Jeffrey is really awesome at basketball, baseball and so much more...

He says he likes fall, summer and spring sports the best.

His very favorite is basketball.

Jeffrey plays on our basketball team

and he is really good at dribbling, shooting and passing.

We teach him good moves and he teaches us.

He always makes baskets and he even blocks some of our shots.

We think he could be a professional basketball player.

He wants to play on the New York Knicks.

Football is Jeffrey's favorite sport to watch.

During football season,

he watches the Jets on live TV all the time.

This is what Jeffrey wrote:

"We watch the game at my house.

My whole family likes the Jets

and can't wait to see them play.

I have a snack like Doritos® and cheer them on.

I like when they kick the ball and make a field goal."

Jeffrey has never been to a real Jets game,

but he really wants to go.

He likes the Jets more than everybody on the planet.

In fact, he was a Jets fan for Halloween.

Jeffrey has Jets everything and

brings his Jets water bottle to school everyday.

NY Jets are the winning team for Jeffrey.

Everyone knows Jeffrey is strong.

It is very hard to beat him at arm wrestling.

For him, it's a piece of cake.

Whenever we arm wrestle with him, he normally wins.

He also gives great big hugs that are very strong.

Jeffrey is also a fast runner.

Very fast.

He has won a lot of gold medals for running.
Every year Jeffrey goes to the Special Olympics where
people with disabilities get to do races and contests.

Jeffrey has a disability called Down syndrome.
He was born with it. It is not contagious and
it doesn't go away like a cold or the flu.
Kids with disabilities are just like you and me
but they do things differently.

All kids are different...

so kids with disabilities are really no different than us.

Just because a kid has Down syndrome
doesn't mean they are not as good at things as we are.
If you ask us, we really don't see any activity
Jeffrey can't do. He is even better at some things than us.
Jeffrey has good handwriting.

He might have the best handwriting in our class.

Jeffrey is a great artist.

He is really good at drawing people.

Jeffrey loves drawing pictures for us,

especially for our classmate, Meadow.

He also drew a picture for Todd on his birthday.

Jeffrey wants to be an artist when he grows up.

We bet $1000 that his artwork will be in a museum.

Jeff loves to sing.

His favorite song is "Baby" by Justin Bieber.

He sings it a lot.

Our gym teacher calls him "JB" which is
short for "Justin Bieber" and "Jeffrey Bill."
When he grows up he wants to be a professional singer
and we believe Jeffrey will be famous.

Jeffrey is a fun kid to be around.

He loves to laugh and listen to jokes.

When we have free time we make up jokes

and he laughs...well, we all laugh.

Jeffrey is really funny too.

He also tells good jokes and makes everybody laugh.

We all laughed when he pretended to be Santa Claus.

We are very lucky to know Jeffrey.

He always wants to hang out with his friends.

He is a great friend and is always there when we need him.

If you met Jeffrey

you would want to be his friend.

When we met Jeffrey,

we didn't know he had Down syndrome.

Most of us were curious and shy,

but some of us were also a little afraid at first

because we didn't know why he looked different.

When someone has Down syndrome, their ears may be small,

their nose might be a little flatter, and their eyes

could be shaped like almonds,

but it does not matter what you look like on the outside.

It matters what you are on the inside

and Jeffrey couldn't be any better than he already is.

Jeffrey is a great boy with a big heart

and should not be treated differently than anyone else.

If someone were ever mean to Jeffrey, we would stick up for him.

Jeffrey has trouble in some of the classes at school
so we help him. Sometimes Jeffrey loses focus
and has a hard time listening.

He needs help getting back on track.

Jeffrey struggles a little bit with following directions.

He just forgets.

We can help him by reminding him

what we should do and when.

Also, we need to repeat directions for him

but it is worth it.

Sometimes it is hard for Jeffrey to learn.

When Jeffrey comes across something challenging for him,

he knows we are always there to help.

You might feel frustrated but you can't be angry

if Jeffrey doesn't get something.

Jeffrey may not learn something the first time

but if you explain and show it to him again,

he will eventually be able to understand the task.

Whatever he is doing, he will not give up.

It's just like when you go to the store and buy two plants.

The one has a beautiful flower and the other has just buds.

The one with only buds on it will grow a pretty flower too.

It will just take a little bit longer.

Jeffrey helps us too.

Just a couple of days ago Hannah wanted a warm cookie.

Hannah couldn't reach it, but Jeffrey just grabbed

the exact one she wanted and gave it to her.

She thanked him and gave him a big hug.

Jeffrey is always there for his friends.

He is very helpful at the end of the day.

If we forget something at school,

like our lunchbox or instrument,

he reads who it belongs to and brings it to us.

Years ago kids with disabilities

were not allowed to go to school.

Who's idea was that?

That was as unfair as slavery.

People didn't believe kids with Down syndrome

could learn the stuff we do, but they can.

It just takes them a little longer.

Keeping kids with disabilities out of school

was an outrage because they are the same as us.

We think that was very unfair

because they couldn't make new friends,

and pursue their hopes and dreams.

You have to have a good education to have a good future.

Now everyone can go to school.

If children like Jeffrey weren't allowed to go to school

we'd be sad and angry.

We would go to the principal and stand up

for all of the kids with disabilities.

It makes us happy nothing will stop

Jeffrey from coming to school, being our friend,

and achieving his goals.

Jeffrey has hopes and dreams and
we are going to encourage him not to give up on them.

We know he can fulfill his dreams.

Jeffrey hopes to go to college
to become a high school teacher.
He wants to teach art, computers, gym and math.
Jeffrey will be a great teacher
because he is great with kids.

Erik thinks Jeffrey will have a huge house
and lots of money. We hope so because
he wants to get married and have 27 kids,
three hamsters and a groundhog.

That's a lot of kids!

Jeffrey also wants to live in a mansion when he can afford it.
Until then, he wants his own room...and a car.

Maybe you will get to meet Jeffrey someday.

We want to know him for the rest of our lives and

hope we meet someone else in the world like Jeffrey.

Get to know people with disabilities.

Don't be scared.

They are just like us!

Children have always been the most accepting of Mikayla's disabilities and the least afraid to ask questions. Understanding is the key to acceptance so I have always given them honest, but sometimes overly complicated answers. Many years ago when a young child asked about Mikayla's feeding tube, Lauren (Mikayla's then three-year-old sister) merely explained, "Mommy feeds Mikayla special milk with a special tube." The boy was clearly satisfied while I would have given too much information, probably leaving the child confused. Being the same age as the child who posed the question, Lauren was able to give just the right answer for his developmental level and understanding. Children are sometimes the best teachers.

Each year, in appreciation for our school's efforts, we purchased books on diversity and disability to donate to the school library. As I searched for new and different books on this topic, with the exception of publications for siblings, I did not find a children's book about disability written by kids. Encouraged by my belief that kids often offer the best explanations for other children, I asked Mikayla's principal and teacher to let me help Mikayla's class write and illustrate a book about having a friend with a disability. Having met her just two years earlier, Mikayla's third-grade classmates knew what it was like to meet and become friends with someone with multiple disabilities. Through their book, Mikayla's friends let other children know it's okay to be afraid when you first meet someone with a disability, but "there is nothing to be scared of." *Our Friend Mikayla* was first published in 2006 and is a valuable tool for teachers and parents who wish to help kids who may be afraid or intimidated upon meeting a disabled child in their school or community. It is an honest and beautiful story about friendship that should be shared with children of all ages.

Motivated by the success of *Our Friend Mikayla*, in 2010 we founded a 501(c)(3) non-profit organization to inspire kids of all abilities to share the message of inclusion. An acronym for the **V**oice **O**f **I**nclusion for **C**hildren **E**verywhere, **Mikayla's Voice** helps children take on projects through which they can share the value and benefits of inclusion. Our projects are as diverse and creative as the kids who create them. We empower children by supporting their ideas, funding their projects, and finding ways to present their work to make certain their message is heard. Through increased inclusive practices in our schools and communities, this generation of children has been blessed with greater appreciation for and friendships with children with disabilities. It is important to help them share the benefits of inclusion so this trend may continue to grow.

On a visit with Mikayla to see her pediatrician, when the receptionist asked about Mikayla's book and our newly-formed organization, I explained how we wanted to help another group of kids write and illustrate a book about their friend with a different disability. She immediately suggested I speak with one of their nurses whose son has Down syndrome and has been included in his school since kindergarten. She contacted Jeffrey's mom who called just a few hours later. After meeting Jeffrey's family, his school principal and fourth grade teachers, it was clear Jeffrey was the perfect subject for a new book. His family embraced the idea and the school was more than willing to allow the time the students would need to work on the project. Most importantly, Jeffrey was comfortable talking about his challenges and enjoyed being the center of attention.

Every moment spent with Jeffrey and his classmates was our honor and privilege. While it is difficult to choose a favorite moment, I do have one discussion I'd like to share. When the kids asked what Down syndrome was, it was difficult for Jeffrey's mom and me to explain. At ten years old, the only "genes" they know are denim blue "jeans." After briefly explaining that genetics determines a person's sex, their eye and hair color, and whether they do or don't have Down syndrome, we asked them to tell us how they might describe Down syndrome to other kids their age. As is always the case, the children rose to our challenge and exceeded our expectations. We featured one of their analogies about flowering plants on page 46, but they had other amazing explanations we wanted to include so you will find them on the next three pages. Enjoy!

~ Kimberly (Mikayla's mom)

A kid with Down syndrome and a kid
without are like two different brands of cell phones.
They are equally cool,
but a little different from each other.

If one race car is not as fast as the others,
it shouldn't make a difference; it's still a race car.
Maybe the race car has better agility
or traction than the others.

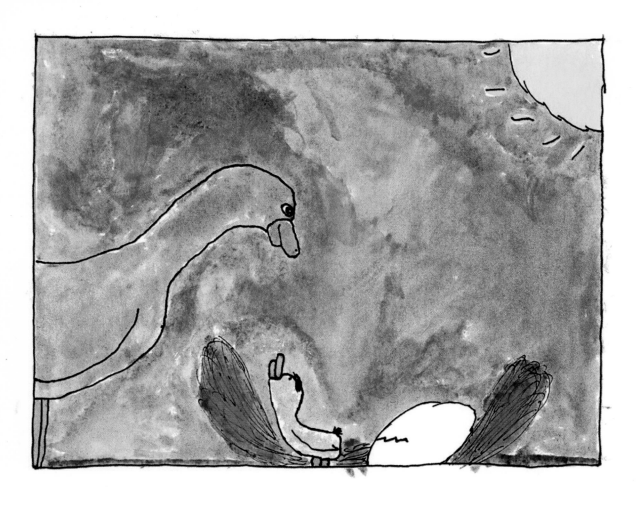

Down syndrome is like if a mother goose has two eggs
and one hatches before the other.
It doesn't mean that the early hatcher is better than the late hatcher.
The mother goose loves them both the same.